Bears, Bears, Bears

Text and Photography by Wayne Lynch

FIREFLY BOOKS

BOOKMAKERS PRESS

To Aubrey,
who gives so much and asks for so little

Canadian Cataloguing in Publication Data

Lynch, Wayne
    Bears, bears, bears

Includes index.
ISBN 1-895565-72-3 (bound)
ISBN 1-895565-69-3 (pbk.)

1. Bears — Juvenile literature.   I. Title.

QL737.C27L9 1995 j599.74'446 C95-931045-2

Front Cover: Polar bears play wrestling.
Photograph by Wayne Lynch.

Back Cover: Brown bears after a swim.
Photograph by Wayne Lynch.

A FIREFLY BOOK

Published by
Firefly Books
250 Sparks Avenue
Willowdale, Ontario
Canada M2H 2S4

Published in the U.S. by
Firefly Books (U.S.) Inc.
P.O. Box 1338, Ellicott Station
Buffalo, New York 14205

Produced by
Bookmakers Press
12 Pine Street
Kingston, Ontario K7K 1W1

Design by
Linda J. Menyes
Q Kumquat Designs

Color separations by
Chroma Graphics (Overseas) Pte. Ltd.
Singapore

Printed and bound in Canada by
Metropole Litho Inc.
St. Bruno de Montarville, Quebec

Printed on acid-free paper

Acknowledgments

Many biologists, too numerous to mention, helped me to understand the complex and intriguing world in which bears live, and I am grateful to all of them.

I am especially indebted, however, to four scientists: Dr. Gary Alt was a friend and adviser throughout the project; Larry Aumiller provided invaluable insight into the bruins of the McNeil River State Game Sanctuary; biologist Peter Clarkson introduced me to the magnificent tundra of Canada's Barren Lands and the grizzlies that roam this vast wilderness; and Dr. Ian Stirling, the most professional and generous scientist I have ever known, was an inspiration and a great help from the beginning, when I first began to observe and study bears 12 years ago.

Bookmakers Press editor Tracy Read deserves special thanks for always believing in this project and for almost always laughing at my jokes. Thanks also to designer Linda Menyes, copy editor Susan Dickinson and proofreader Catherine DeLury.

Contents

Introduction

When I was a boy, I was terrified of bears. Every year, I spent the summer holidays helping my uncle on his dairy farm in southern Ontario. At that time, black bears still roamed the woods bordering the fields around the farm. Although I never saw a bear during those summers, I heard many stories that bolstered their savage reputation.

None of those stories, however, prepared me for the dread I felt when I finally saw my first wild bear. My family and I were picnicking beside a waterfall in northern Ontario. All afternoon, I had teased my parents and younger brother, insisting that I had seen a bear in the bushes. I urged them over and over again to come and see for themselves. I loved how excited they became, then I would laugh and tell them it was just a joke.

Later, as I stood alone beside the river, the bushes on the far shore began to move. I couldn't believe my eyes when a big black bear stepped out into the open. I had never seen such a large animal. The bear strolled along the riverbank plucking blueberries from the bushes with its floppy lips. I was frozen in my tracks and too afraid to make a peep. I watched the bear for several minutes until it disappeared into the woods. Then I ran back to tell my family, but of course, no one believed me.

If a fortune-teller had told me then that when I grew up, I would spend more than 10 years learning everything I could about bears—reading each new book and article I could get my hands on, crawling inside the winter dens of black bears and polar bears, holding squirming grizzly cubs in my arms and capturing on film black bears, brown bears and polar bears doing everything from fishing to fighting—I never would have believed it. But that's exactly what happened.

My search for these animals took me on an around-the-world odyssey. In the end, I would travel over 240,000

Bear Facts

More than 400,000 black bears live in North America, a population greater than that of the other seven bear species combined.

—

The koala bear is not really a bear at all but a marsupial, which carries its young inside a pouch on its belly.

—

The polar bear, the youngest species of bear, evolved from the brown bear during the last Ice Age, 250,000 years ago.

---

kilometers (150,000 mi), on four different continents. My quest for bears has given me some of the greatest experiences of my life, and along the way, I've learned a great deal about them. I no longer believe bears are bloodthirsty killers lurking in the woods waiting to attack anyone who comes along. Large, powerful animals that are capable of defending themselves with tooth and claw, bears spend a lot more time trying to avoid encounters with people than they do stalking and attacking them.

Like many fears, my childhood fear of bears was rooted in ignorance. The more I learn about bears, the less I fear them. In fact, today I am more frightened of the things that *people* can do to me than I am of bears.

The accomplished lecturer Helen Keller, who also happened to be deaf and blind, said that "life can be a daring adventure or nothing at all." My search for bears made my life what I want it to be. In this book, I want to share with you some of the strange and wonderful facts I've been able to learn about the lives of bears, things that most people don't know. I want you to be thrilled, as I am, at the prospect of seeing a bear in the wild, and together, I hope we can work to protect these magnificent creatures and the wilderness they inhabit.

Its shoulder hump distinguishes the brown bear from the other northern bears. The hump consists of well-developed shoulder muscles that the animal uses when digging.

What Is a Bear?

It's easy to become confused when you try to figure out how animals are related. Animals that have absolutely no genetic connection sometimes display very similar behaviors or physical characteristics. Today, scientists rely on complicated blood tests to determine which animals belong to which animal family. Everyone now agrees that bears belong to the group of mammals we call carnivores, a group that includes such familiar animals as dogs, cats, raccoons, skunks and hyenas. These are the relatives of bears, and surprisingly, the closest of the relatives is the raccoon.

Eight different kinds, or species, of bears inhabit the world today. They can be divided into two groups: the northern bears, which include the brown bear, the polar bear, the American black bear and the Asiatic black bear; and the tropical bears, which include the sloth bear, the sun bear, the spectacled bear and the giant panda.

Bears are extremely adaptable animals and can therefore be found in a wide range of environments, from Arctic tundra to tropical rainforests. If you refer to the map on page 60, you will see that the greatest variety of bears, six of the eight species, live in Asia. You will also notice that only one of the bears, the spectacled bear, lives south of the equator, in the high-elevation cloud forests of the Andes Mountains of South America.

Bulky Bears

What exactly is it about its appearance that makes a bear look like a bear? All bears have big heads, little eyes and relatively small, rounded ears. They have large, muscular bodies with thick, strong legs. Even the smallest of the bears, the sun bear of Southeast Asia, weighs around 45 kilograms (100 lb), while the largest, the polar bear and the brown bear, may weigh more than 450 kilograms (1,000 lb). The five other bear species are medium in weight and average between 68 and 136 kilograms (150-300 lb).

The largest polar bear ever weighed tipped the scales at 800 kilograms (1,764 lb). Such an animal may well have been over 3 meters (10 ft) long, from the tip of its black, wet nose to the end of its short, stubby tail, and over 1.5 meters (5 ft) tall at the shoulder. When this huge polar bear reared up on its hind legs, it might easily have stood over 3.5 meters (11½ ft) tall—a full meter (3 ft) higher than the average ceiling in your house.

The biggest bear I've ever seen was Bart, a tame brown bear that has appeared in numerous films and television shows. Originally from Kodiak Island, Alaska, Bart starred in the popular movie *The Bear*, which was released in 1989. His owner and trainer, Doug Seus, reports that the 20-year-old bear weighs over 680 kilograms (1,500 lb). He reached that size by indulging in his favorite foods: pot roast with lots of garlic for the main course and can after can of Hawaiian Punch to wash it all down.

Footwear and Fingernails

All bears walk on the soles of their feet, just as humans do, rather than on their toes, as most carnivores do. A

Bear Facts

Because of their rich diet of salmon, the brown bears that live along the coast of Alaska and in Kamchatka, Russia, are the largest in the world.

—

Bears have such small eyes that people often assume they must also have poor eyesight, but bears probably see as well as many humans.

—

Tipping the scales at 365 kilograms (805 lb), an American black bear from Manitoba is the largest ever weighed.

Its sense of smell is probably more important to a bear than either its eyes or its ears. Like all bears, this cinnamon-colored American black bear relies on its nose to find food and to identify other bears.

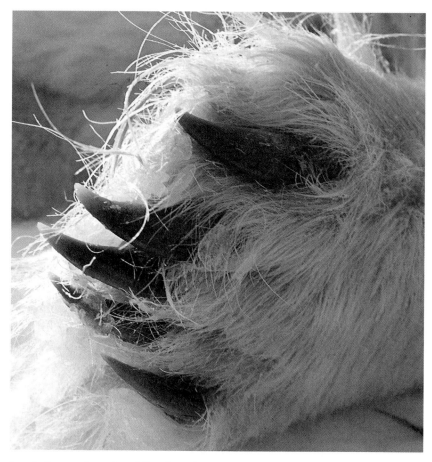

During winter hibernation, northern bears shed the skin from the soles of their feet, sometimes eating the sloughed-off skin.

The polar bear, on the other hand, is at the opposite end of the scale when it comes to footwear. Its soles are almost completely covered with fur, which provides insulation against the cold snow. The small bit of skin that is not covered with fur is roughened like coarse sandpaper to prevent slipping.

When viewed under a microscope, the black skin of a polar bear's foot pad is covered with thousands of tiny bumps. This antiskid feature was discovered by a group of British researchers with the Ford Motor Company, who were trying to develop slip-resistant footwear to reduce industrial accidents. Their findings led them to produce a soft shoe soling that was covered with small bumps similar to the foot pads of a polar bear.

The soles of the three other species show a combination of fur and bare skin. The foot diversity we see in bears is a good example of how evolution works. Over many millions of years, each bear species has developed the footwear that best suits its environment and its life style.

Evolution is also responsible for the type of claws bears have. All bears have five heavy curved claws

bear's feet are broad and flat. Its soles may be covered with varying amounts of fur or may be completely bare. For example, the Asiatic black bear, the sloth bear, the spectacled bear and the sun bear all live in forest habitats where they must often clamber up tall trees in search of food. If they were to slip and fall while climbing, they could be seriously injured. Consequently, none of these bears have fur on the soles of their feet, so they are able to get a better grip on wet, slippery tree trunks and branches.

Bears, such as this female brown bear, sit on the ground and stand upright, just as we do. In ancient times, these similarities to humans convinced many people that bears were sacred animals.

on each foot. Both the sloth bear and the brown bear (also known as the grizzly bear) have especially powerful front claws that can be nine centimeters (3½ in) long. Researchers found one large brown bear with claws the length of a ballpoint pen—

imagine having fingernails that long!

Because the sloth bear and the brown bear do lots of digging, they have evolved large front claws. The sloth bear unearths termites and ants, while the brown bear digs up the juicy roots of plants as well as the tunnels

of rodents such as ground squirrels.

What is a bear? Among many other things, a bear is a big, fat flat-footed carnivore with chubby legs, small beady eyes, a stubby tail and dirty fingernails. But I dare anyone to say that to its face.

9

A Coat of Many Colors

When compared with tropical birds or with the spectacular iridescent fish on a coral reef, most bears are not very colorful. One exception is the giant panda, which is easily recognized because of the striking black and white pattern of its fur.

Half of the world's bears, including the Asiatic black bear, the sloth bear, the sun bear and the spectacled bear, have plain blackish fur with the occasional light patch on their faces, throats or upper chests. The sun bear, the sloth bear and the Asiatic black bear frequently boast a white, orange or yellowish patch on their upper chests. In fact, the light-colored V-shaped pattern on the Asiatic black bear's chest is so distinctive that some people call this bear the moon bear, because the marking resembles a crescent moon. The throat and chest markings on all these bears are easiest to see when the animals sit up on their haunches or stand on their hind legs.

The markings on the spectacled bear, however, are quite different. The bear originally acquired its name because of the noticeable pale-colored circles or semicircles around its eyes, which resemble eyeglasses. The white or yellowish markings may sometimes spread across the animal's cheeks and down onto its throat. Though the shape and color of the markings vary

greatly from bear to bear, those on an individual bear do not change throughout its life.

Everyone knows that a polar bear's fur is white, but there are minor differences between animals. Polar bears range in color from silvery white to pale yellow. Newborn cubs are always pure white, but some polar bears, especially adult males, turn yellow as they get older.

The first time I saw the purplish black tongue of a polar bear, I immediately assumed the bear was sick. It turns out that unlike other bears, a polar bear has black skin—even on the inside of its mouth. Although no one knows for certain why a polar

---

Bear Facts

Most bears molt their fur once each year, during the summer.

—

The thick, woolly coat of the giant panda is oily and helps keep the bear's skin from getting wet.

—

Because the thinnest fur is on its belly, a polar bear cools off in the summer by stretching out on a patch of ice or snow.

---

bear has black skin instead of pink, scientists speculate that the dark color may help the bear absorb a little more heat from the sun. For an animal that spends most of its life in a harsh winter climate, such an adaptation makes a lot of sense.

Names That Can Fool You

Here's a riddle: Which species of bear is sometimes brown and sometimes blond, and when it is white or blue, it is *still* black? The answer? The American black bear.

Let me explain. The American black bear got its name because in most areas where it is found in North America and Mexico, its fur is black. But the American black bear is not always black. In western Canada and the western United States, many black bears are chocolate brown, cinnamon or even blond. In fact, in some states in the American Southwest, such as Arizona, most black bears are different shades of brown; only a very few actually have black fur.

In the rainforests of coastal British Columbia, there is a small population of black bears whose fur is completely white—even their claws are ivory-colored! The aboriginal peoples call them spirit bears. Not all black bears in this part of North America are white, however. Most of them still

Found along the coast of British Columbia, the spirit bear is actually an American black bear with white fur. The spirit bear is not an albino; it has brown eyes and a black nose, as do all black bears.

The sun bear of Southeast Asia has the shortest fur of any bear on Earth. Because its body isn't hidden beneath a thick coat of fur, the sun bear looks very muscular.

have black fur. Spirit bears are rare, and they live among the far more numerous black-colored bears. Sometimes a black mother bear may have one white cub and one black cub; sometimes all the cubs of a white mother bear may be black.

In southeastern Alaska, just north of where the spirit bear roams, there is yet another black bear that does not have black fur. Sometimes called the blue bear, or glacier bear, this bear has silver-gray or bluish black fur. Like the white spirit bear, the blue bear is rare.

Now let's look at brown bears. Are brown bears always brown, or do they also come in different colors? Brown bears vary in color from blond to dark brown, and the tips of their fur are sometimes whitish in color, which gives the animal a "frosted" appearance. This frosted brown bear is often called a silvertip.

One final tidbit, something with which to quiz your friends. How many kinds of brown bears are there? If you look at the map on page 60, you'll see that the brown bear makes its home in a greater number of diverse regions around the world than does any other bear. Not surprisingly, then, this bear has acquired different names, depending on where it lives. Among the names given to the brown bear are

Kodiak bear, coastal brown bear, Kamchatka bear, Alaskan brownie, yeso bear and silvertip; yet all these bears are the same animal. Even the infamous grizzly bear is not a different bear; it is simply another name for the brown bear. How many kinds of brown bears are there? Just one.

Coat Exchange

As with all mammals, a bear's coat becomes bleached and worn over time, and as a result, a northern bear molts and replaces its entire coat every summer. It takes a lot of energy to replace all of the fur on a bear, so the first bears to molt are those animals with the largest energy reserves; namely, adult males. Adult male brown bears, for example, begin to molt and look shaggy by the first week of July, and most finish molting by the middle of August.

The bears with the smallest energy reserves are mother bears with nursing cubs. Mother bears must molt and also continue to supply milk to their growing cubs. In an effort to conserve much-needed energy, females with cubs molt more gradually than adult males. Mother brown bears usually begin to molt several weeks later than adult males, and they often are not finished molting until the middle of September.

A Bear's Neighborhood

I once thought that bears simply wandered around aimlessly, traveling wherever they wanted, searching for food and shelter and never staying in one place for too long. But after spending more than 10 years studying bears, I now know that they are not like that at all. In fact, every bear spends its life within a relatively well-defined area, a piece of land that is much like what a neighborhood is to you and me. A bear's neighborhood, however, is often very large—sometimes hundreds of square kilometers—and the bear stays in that neighborhood for most of its life. People, especially people with sophisticated transportation systems, tend to move around a lot more than the average bear.

Modern technology has played an important role in helping us to discover such secrets about bears. Today, a researcher can track a bear's movements with a piece of equipment called a radio-collar. A radio-collar is a thick belt made of plastic, rubber and leather with a small radio transmitter, about the size of your fist, taped to it. After the bear has been temporarily slowed down with a tranquilizer dart, researchers strap the radio-collar around its neck. When the bear is back on its feet and begins to travel from one place to another, the radio sends out a signal that is re-ceived by an antenna. Nowadays, the antenna may be located on a satellite circling high above Earth.

Once a satellite antenna receives a signal from a radio-collared bear, the information is sent back to Earth to the researcher, who can then pinpoint the bear's location on a map. As the location changes, the researcher is able to follow the animal's movements on the map. By tracking the bear in this way for several years, the researcher can develop a fairly good idea of how much space the bear will use in its lifetime and which areas are most important to the animal's survival.

There's a good chance that the equipment used to monitor a bear's movements may one day also be used to keep track of you and me. Just as many people now carry "beepers" with them wherever they go, some scientists predict that in the future, everyone will carry a "personal locater." This miniature device would work just like a bear's radio-collar, only you would carry it in your pocket.

Home on the Range: Bigger Is Not Better

It makes a lot of sense for a bear to live in the smallest area it can. That way, it doesn't waste a lot of energy traveling great distances for no reason. At the same time, the bear becomes familiar with the best feeding spots in its neighborhood, and it knows the safest places to hide if it needs to escape from danger. Also, when winter comes, the bear has already discovered trees, caves and other spots in which to hibernate.

Indeed, bears everywhere tend to live in the smallest area they can. Instead of calling this area a neighborhood, however, scientists refer to it as an animal's "home range." Each bear has a home range, but the size and shape of the home range is different for almost every bear. Some may be the size of a small town, while others, like the home range of the polar bear, may be twice as large as a country the size of Iceland.

Bear Facts

The home range of a polar bear may cover an area twice the size of Iceland.

—

A male bear's home range usually overlaps those of two or more female bears.

—

Young female bears sometimes inherit part of their mother's home range.

A ndy Derocher fits a mother
polar bear with a satellite radio-
collar. This device allows scientists
to track the movements of polar
bears even as they travel thousands
of kilometers over the sea ice.

Polar bears have the largest home range of any bear. The home range of just one polar bear in Alaska was found to be 45 times greater than the area of Great Smoky Mountains National Park in Tennessee, which is home to some 400 black bears.

One of the main factors determining the size of a bear's home range is the amount of food it is able to find. Brown bears in the Brooks Mountains of northern Alaska, for example, may need a home range of more than 1,300 square kilometers (500 sq mi), because food in this area is so scarce and poor in quality. These bears eat mostly roots, grasses and berries. Now and then, they might chance upon a ground squirrel or a caribou calf. Compare this diet with that of brown bears making their homes farther south on Kodiak Island, Alaska, where the living is easy. Some of the Kodiak brown bears need less than 25 square kilometers (10 sq mi) of home range, because the food there, which includes fresh salmon, is so abundant and nutritious.

The availability of food affects the size of not only a bear's home range but also the bear itself. A large male brown bear from the Brooks Mountains could weigh about 275 kilograms (600 lb), while a big, burly brown bear from Kodiak Island might tip the scales at more than 550 kilograms (1,200 lb)!

Day Beds and Bear Trails

Have you ever been hiking through the woods and suddenly noticed a bear track in the mud along the trail?

16

If you're anything like me, your heart instantly begins to beat faster. Even though the track may be many days old, you'll look around to see whether the bear is still nearby. In our imaginations, the bear is such a formidable animal that the slightest hint we've been anywhere near one can get the adrenaline flowing. That's the way I feel when I spot any one of the different bear signs scattered throughout a bear's home range. Stumbling upon such signs can be almost as thrilling as sighting the bear itself.

Bears are not active 24 hours a day, even when they are having a tough time finding the food they require. As a result, they sometimes rest for many hours at night and take frequent naps during the day. When the bear wants to rest, it often makes a day bed.

A day bed is usually easy to recognize. It is either a low mound of dried grasses, leaves and conifer needles raked into a pile by the bear from the surrounding forest floor or a shallow hole dug into the ground and scraped clean of vegetation. A bear may have seven or eight day beds in a favorite area. Day beds are often built in thick vegetation, where not only is it cooler but the bear is hidden from the view of passersby. A black bear sometimes builds its day bed at the base of a large tree. When danger threatens, the bear can scramble up the tree to safety.

Well-trodden trails are another sign to look for in bear country. Bears, like humans, are creatures of habit and frequently use the same trails over and over again to move from one place to another. There are several different kinds of bear trails. Often, the trail is simply a single rut in the ground, usually a few centimeters deep. In rare cases, the ruts may be as much as a meter (3 ft) deep. Trails such as these have, over many years, been worn deeper and deeper by hundreds of bears traversing them.

The most interesting trail I ever discovered was in the coastal rainforest of British Columbia. It consisted of a series of large, well-defined footprints—footprints that sank into the earth as if made by the legendary Big Foot, the giant, hairy apelike being said to roam these ancient forests. In fact, the trail had been made by generations of bears that had stepped into the same footprints each time they traveled through the forest. Eventually, the tracks became deeper and wider. I suspect that such bear trails have served as the "evidence" which has led people to believe in the legend of Big Foot in the first place.

17

The Mating Season

Unlike many members of the animal kingdom, including humans, adult male and female bears do not live together throughout the year. In fact, adult bears typically spend much of their lives traveling alone, except, of course, when a mother bear is with her cubs. As a result, one of the most important times of the year for bears is the spring mating season. Without it, there would be no more bears.

Although bears are loners, most of them share part of their home range with other bears. From time to time, they run into their neighbors, but typically, they try to avoid each other. All of that changes, however, during the mating season. Suddenly, male and female bears need to get together.

The tropical sun bear mates throughout the year, but all the other bears breed between April and July. In North America, June is the peak mating period for black bears and brown bears. Among the four northern species, the adult male is usually larger than the female, sometimes weighing twice as much. In polar bears, the weight difference can be even greater, with a large male weighing as much as three times more than the female.

Because they are smaller, females are generally frightened of male bears—and with good reason. Male bears have been known to kill females for food. Consequently, it takes some time for a female bear to learn to trust a male suitor during the mating season. At the beginning of courtship, a male bear will simply follow a female at a distance until she allows him to come close enough to communicate his peaceful intentions.

In time, the female bear relaxes and the male makes contact. As the courtship progresses, the two bears may nuzzle and chew on each other's head and neck; they may even wrestle and play a little. Eventually, the bears mate, which they will do three or four times a day for several days. Then,

Bear Facts

Bears may mate with more than one partner throughout the breeding season.

—

During the mating season, adult male bears may kill cubs.

—

Even though bears mate in spring, the babies do not begin to develop inside the mother's body until autumn, a remarkable adaptation called delayed implantation.

abruptly, the pair separates. Afterward, the male and female resume their solitary lives. From that day on, the male will take no responsibility for raising his cubs.

Battling Bears

There is a reason why male northern bears are so much larger than females. The bigger and more powerful the male, the better his chances of mating with the female bears in his neighborhood, because he can easily shove around smaller male bears. The action really heats up when two males are interested in the same female. In the bear world, as in the human world, that usually results in a fight.

During the mating season, it's not uncommon to see males with fresh cuts on their heads, necks and shoulders. One spring, I was able to examine an adult male polar bear up close. The bear had deep puncture wounds on its left shoulder, half of its right ear had been torn off, and the fourth claw on its left front paw had been ripped out. There were also several old scars on its nose and forehead.

Dr. Lynn Rogers, a bear biologist from Minnesota, has watched rival male black bears fight many times. In the fights where one male bear was much larger than the other, the larger bear simply chased away his smaller

Rival adult male polar bears may fight furiously during the spring mating season. The bears target each other's face and neck, accessible and vulnerable areas. Deep lacerations and broken canine teeth are relatively frequent injuries, and sometimes the bears' jaws are even broken.

opponent. The real battles occurred when the contestants were about the same size. Sometimes the bears would fight for several minutes, clawing and biting each other repeatedly, occasionally even breaking their large canine teeth. The fighting area became trampled and littered with broken vegetation and clumps of fur. When the struggle finally ended, both the winner and the loser usually limped off nursing their wounds.

Male bears may use another tactic besides fighting to ensure success during the mating season. Researchers have observed male polar bears and male brown bears using physical intimidation to kidnap females. In the polar bear population, courting males appear to drive females into small bays or onto hillsides, away from areas of sea ice where most other bears—in particular, potential male rivals—are hunting seals.

In the case of the brown bear, a female was herded into a small valley high in the mountains, where she was held hostage by the male. Out of the sight of potential male competitors, the male bear simply waited for the female to become receptive and then mated with her. By keeping the female in a remote area, the male bear avoided having to fight for her with larger males and risk serious injury.

During mating, brown bears may remain coupled for up to 30 minutes, and they may mate three or four times within a 24-hour period.

Bear Chow

Bears are like humans. They eat almost everything, from clams and raw fish to nuts, fruits and berries. And let's not forget juicy red meat. Nothing satisfies a bear more than a hearty meal of fresh caribou, moose or deer. Some bears may even tackle the occasional dull-witted cow, but that kind of meal almost always gets a bear into trouble.

Although all bears appear to love a meaty meal, their diet is usually more like that of cattle than of carnivores. Green vegetation such as grasses, sedges, tree leaves and wildflowers are the main food of many bears. The giant panda, for example, eats practically nothing but bamboo leaves and shoots. Even macho grizzly bears eat greenery much of the time.

Bears are very good at sniffing out the most nutritious foods in their home range. Nothing is too crunchy or slimy for them to eat. Grizzly bears (remember, this is just another name for the brown bear) in Yellowstone National Park, in Wyoming, search the meadows and forests for dried buffalo droppings. With a quick flip of a paw, the bears overturn the chips and lick up the crickets, beetles and worms hiding underneath. In the eastern United States, American black bears climb into trees to rip open the silk nests of tent caterpillars, then gobble up the hundreds of exposed squirming larvae.

Insects are everywhere, so it's not surprising that they are eaten by many different bears. Both Asiatic and American black bears tear apart old tree stumps and decaying logs to feast on the beetle grubs living inside. In Borneo, daredevil sun bears climb high into trees to plunder the nests of wild bees for honey and wiggly white larvae. This habit has earned the sun bear the local name of honey bear. In Norway, brown bears destroy anthills with a few swipes of their long claws and lap up the ants as they scurry out to defend their nests. After they've snacked, the enterprising bears use the flattened anthills as day beds.

Among bears, though, the insect specialist must certainly be the sloth bear, whose primary taste is for termites. A sloth bear is a termite's worst nightmare. The bear's long claws enable it to tear open even the hardest sunbaked termite mound. Its floppy lips are ideal for capturing fleeing termites, and its nose has very little fur on it, so it doesn't get gummed up with the sticky glue sprayed by angry termites. The bear can even close its nostrils to prevent soldier termites from invading and launching a counterattack. Best of all, the sloth bear happens to be missing two upper front teeth, so its lips and mouth act like the hose of a vacuum cleaner, sucking up the tasty termites. Vacuum cleaners are not very quiet, nor is the sloth bear when it is eating. Local people can often locate the bear by the loud huffing and puffing noises it makes as it ingests termites.

One of the unusual foods that bears eat is tree bark. I expected porcupines, squirrels and rabbits to chew on trees, but never bears. Brown bears, as well as American and Asiatic black bears, strip the outer bark from trees with their teeth and then scrape off the

Bear Facts

Brown bears in coastal Alaska may swim up to 16 kilometers (10 mi) offshore to feast on seabird colonies.

—

A group of 75 polar bears was once observed feeding on the carcasses of three bowhead whales on the north coast of Alaska.

—

A giant panda eats an average of 12.5 kilograms (28 lb) of bamboo leaves and stems every day and produces over 100 droppings.

A black bear tears apart rotten logs and tree stumps to feast on insect larvae. The bear locates the insects using its keen sense of smell.

In the spring, brown bears love to feed on sedges. Bears are experts at locating the most nutritious foods in their home range, and at this time of the year, sedges may contain as much as 25 percent protein.

tracks in western Montana, spilling tons of corn beside the rails. The huge pile of corn quickly began to ferment, and the area smelled like a beer parlor. The bears discovered it.

Like dopey boozers, as many as a dozen drunken bears, both blacks and grizzlies, could soon be seen sitting on their butts around the corn pile. The situation became dangerous when dazed bears began to wander in front of oncoming trains. Railroad workers, desperate to get rid of the bears, tried to discourage them by covering the corn with dirt and mixing in lime to make the corn taste bad. Nothing stopped the bears, which continued to return to the pile of corn over the next five years. I guess they found it hard to kick the habit.

Down at the Old Fishing Hole

Bears, especially North American bears, never pass up an opportunity to go fishing. Black bears in Alberta and Saskatchewan fish for white suckers in the spring, while black bears in Quebec go after doré. In Wyoming and Montana, brown bears wade into shallow streams in the summer to catch cutthroat trout. But there is one type of fish that, above all others, is a favorite with brown and black bears alike: the Pacific salmon.

Each year, millions of salmon mi-

spongy, sugary white sapwood underneath. In Japan and western North America, bears with this kind of sweet tooth get into lots of trouble with the forest industry. Stripping the bark from a tree sometimes kills the tree; at the very least, it allows insects and diseases to invade it, weakening the tree and stunting its growth. Either way, foresters are always unhappy with bark-eating bears.

Bears can get into other kinds of trouble because of the foods they eat. One year, two railroad cars ran off the

Brown bears use several dozen different methods to catch salmon. Yearling cubs, such as these triplets, accompany their mother into the river to learn the fishing techniques that are most successful.

grate from the open ocean to northern coastlines on both sides of the Pacific Ocean, especially in Alaska, British Columbia, Washington and eastern Russia. The salmon in these areas swim upstream, sometimes traveling more than a thousand kilometers (600 mi) to reach the shallow rivers and creeks where they mate, lay their eggs, then die. Near the end of their journey, the salmon meet the bears.

Salmon are strong swimmers, so the black bears and brown bears that fish for them frequently choose areas where it is a little tougher for the fish to escape. A popular fishing spot for bears is a waterfall, where the salmon are slowed down as they try to jump up the falls to continue upstream.

Like humans who fish, bears use many different methods to catch salmon. Some snorkel at the base of the falls and try to trap salmon between their front legs or catch a sluggish fish in their mouths. Others fish downstream, splashing around to drive the panicky salmon into shallow water, where they are easier to catch.

The most common way for a bear to go fishing is simply to stand in the current and wait for a fish to swim within reach. Sometimes a bear positions itself at the upper edge of the falls and catches a salmon in midair as the fish leaps up. Three or four fish may jump at once, however, which can confuse the bear so much that it misses all of them.

Occasionally, the bear doesn't notice the jumping salmon until the fish hits it in the butt or crashes into the side of its head. The surprised bear then looks around quickly as though checking to see whether any other bears happened to notice its clumsiness.

Bears are patient fishers, and they often catch their limit. I have seen brown bears harvest up to 10 salmon in an hour. In the McNeil River State Game Sanctuary, in Alaska, a bear can catch as many as 50 salmon a day. The record belongs to a large brown bear named Groucho, whose personal best was 88 chum salmon in a single day. That summer, he caught a total of 1,018 salmon! How did he eat so many fish?

Groucho weighed over 450 kilograms (1,000 lb), but even a bear that size would have trouble eating 1,000 salmon. A chum salmon typically weighs 2.5 to 4.5 kilograms (5½-10 lb), which would have meant that on his best day, Groucho ate at least 200 kilograms (440 lb) of fish. Even a chowhound like Groucho couldn't manage that.

*A*t the peak of the salmon spawn-
ing run, a brown bear can catch
over a dozen fish in an hour. The
bear may eat the salmon right there
or carry it into the bushes, out of the
sight of other bears. Since bears
steal fish from one another, such
secrecy lessens the chance of piracy.

When a bear catches more salmon
than it can consume, which happens
often, it becomes a very fussy eater. It
devours only its favorite parts of the
salmon: the brain and head, the skin
and the eggs. These fat-rich morsels
produce the most energy. Once the
bear has eaten them, the rest of the
fish is left for scavengers, such as
ravens, gulls, eagles and other bears.

As it turns out, bears get rid of the
very parts of the salmon that people
like—the bright red meat—while we
usually turn up our noses at the parts
the bears prefer. As I was returning to
my camp one afternoon in Alaska, I
spotted a skinned, headless salmon
floating downstream from a waterfall
where I knew brown bears were fishing. I scooped up the fish for dinner.
That salmon was the best I had ever
eaten. Just knowing the fish had been
caught by a bear made the meal that
much tastier.

Nanuk, the Seal Hunter
Although a polar bear may eat berries
and even seaweed, it eats meat most
of the time. In fact, the polar bear eats
more meat than any other bear—raw
seal meat, day in and day out; a rather
boring diet.

Watching polar bears hunt seals in
the high Arctic was one of the most
thrilling experiences of my life. My tent

In winter, the sea ice cracks and piles into ridges, and ringed seals dig caves in the snowdrifts that form along the ridges. A common polar bear hunting technique is to follow these ridges, searching out seals.

was set up on a high cliff overlooking the frozen sea. Each night when I went to bed, my sleeping bag felt like an icebox, but I was happy, because all day long, I could watch bears.

Polar bears use two different methods to catch seals: still-hunting and stalk-ing. A still-hunting bear either stands or lies beside a seal's breathing hole and waits, while a stalking bear spots the seal, then tries to sneak up on it.

Seals are air-breathing mammals like humans, and even though a seal is well adapted for a life in the water, it must come up for a breath of air three or four times an hour. The problem for the polar bear is that a seal often has several breathing holes from which to choose. The bear must be patient—and a little bit lucky—if it is to catch the seal.

This newborn ringed seal pup was killed by a polar bear. The bear may not have been very hungry at the time, since it ate only the fat-rich skin and blubber and abandoned the rest of the carcass.

A still-hunting polar bear must also be very quiet while it waits for a seal to poke its head through the hole. If the bear shuffles its feet or accidentally scrapes its claws on the ice, the seal may hear it underwater and swim to another hole. After a couple of hours, the bear may give up. It might even fall asleep.

When a polar bear gets lucky, though, the hunt is over quickly. In an instant, the bear grabs the seal's head with its teeth and, using its well-developed muscles, drags the seal up through the breathing hole onto the ice. The seal dies almost immediately.

The best hunting season is from April to July, when the seals are young and inexperienced. On average, a polar bear kills a seal every five or six days, but in the high Arctic, I watched a female teenage bear kill four seals in less than two days. We called this bear the "killing machine." After it killed the last seal, the bear played with the dead animal for nearly 20 minutes. Six times, it dragged the carcass back to the breathing hole and dropped it into the water. Each time, it would haul the seal's body back onto the ice and stand over it for a couple of minutes. After eating very little of it, the bear left.

When a polar bear catches more seals than it can eat, it consumes only the fat-rich parts of the seal, much

like the brown bear that sometimes eats only the fat-rich parts of a salmon. In a seal, most of the fat is in the blubber and skin. The bears leave the rest of the carcass lying on the ice for scavengers. Arctic foxes often follow the trail of a hunting polar bear for just this reason.

In June, most seals come up onto the ice to warm themselves in the sun. They need the warmth of the sun to shed their winter coats, and they may lie on the ice for 24 hours or more at a stretch. At this time of year, seals are most vulnerable to stalking bears.

A polar bear must be very crafty to

catch a seal on the ice, because the seals are constantly sniffing the wind and looking around for danger. What makes it even more challenging for the bear is that the seals may haul out in groups of a hundred or more along a crack in the ice, so there are that many more noses and eyes trying to detect a stalking bear.

To approach a seal, the stalking bear crouches down and slowly creeps ahead, hiding behind chunks of ice when it can. It may also slip into deep pools of meltwater and carefully paddle closer. When the bear is within 20 or 30 meters (65-100 ft) of the unsuspecting seal, it charges. Seals have very fast reflexes, so more often than not, they escape.

Sometimes a polar bear will actually swim under the ice to catch the seal off guard by coming up through a breathing hole. The bear pops out right next to the resting seal. That's what you call fast-food takeout, bear-style.

Hunting Muskoxen, Moose and Deer

The polar bear is not the only bear that hunts for meat. Brown bears, American black bears and sometimes Asiatic black bears hunt whenever an opportunity presents itself.

Young hoofed mammals, such as elk, muskoxen, deer, moose and caribou,

A walrus is the largest animal a polar bear can kill. A bull walrus may weigh over 900 kilograms (1,980 lb), and its long tusks make it dangerous to attack. Nonetheless, a polar bear is sometimes able to kill this powerful marine mammal by biting it around its head and face.

are born in late spring. In late June, brown bears in the Canadian Rockies head for certain parts of the mountains because they know that this is when and where elk calves are usually born. In Yellowstone National Park, the brown bears snoop their way across the meadows searching for the calves they know are hiding in the grass and shrubbery. In some other regions of North America, bears end up killing nearly half of the newborn elk calves.

Brown bears can run fast, up to 40 kilometers per hour (25 mph), but they tire quickly, and most chases last less than 100 meters (325 ft). In Alaska, a fleet-footed grizzly may charge into a herd of caribou. As the animals scatter, the bear will grab a young calf. Black bears in Newfoundland prey on caribou calves in much the same way.

Baby animals aren't the only ones that are hunted by bears. A bear may even stalk a 450-kilogram (1,000 lb) bull moose. At the end of the rutting season, adult bull moose are exhausted and weak after fighting each other for females. When the moose are tired like this, the bears can attack and kill them more easily. Bull caribou and elk are also weakened by the battles of their autumn rut, and bears hunt them as well.

Late winter is another time when animals are easier prey for bears. After months of poor food and difficult weather, many deer and elk are so weakened that researchers call them "the walking dead," because the animals eventually die of starvation before the winter is over. Animals like these are sometimes the first meal that a bear will have when it comes out of its winter den. Coastal bears might dine on skunk cabbage, seaweed and mussels.

Researchers still agree that most brown bears and black bears are mainly vegetarians, but these animals can also be skilled predators whenever they have the chance.

Food That Fights Back

The battle between bears and the food they eat sometimes has a way of backfiring on the bears.

A few years ago, biologist Tom Barry watched as five brown bears raided the wild goose colony he was studying in the Canadian Arctic. Over 6,000 nests were destroyed. Barry estimated that the bears had probably gulped down more than 24,000 eggs, shells and all. He was furious at the bears but seemed happy to report that most of the bears suffered terrible bouts of diarrhea as a result of devouring all those rich eggs.

From time to time, black bears in the Okefenokee Swamp of southern Georgia get into trouble with another egg-laying animal. Alligator nests are often raided by black bears, and sometimes the toothy reptiles get even. In one case, a 2.5-meter (8 ft) alligator attacked a juvenile black bear while the bear was swimming in a pond. Halfway across, the alligator grabbed the bear and pulled it underwater, but the bear struggled free and escaped to shore with little more than a limp to show for the attack.

Other black bears have not been so lucky. There are many tales, not all of them tall, told by old "swampers"—people who have lived in the swamps all their lives—of big bull alligators, 3.5 meters (11½ ft) or more in length, dragging bears under the water. The bears are never seen again.

Porcupines are another risky food that black bears, brown bears and even polar bears occasionally try to eat. Most of the bears quickly learn that the five-kilogram (11 lb) porky is better left alone. A nose full of quills is a painful lesson a bear does not soon forget, and a front paw full of quills can keep a bear on three legs for weeks. Even so, some bears persist in tackling the prickly porcupine time and time again.

One female brown bear near a salmon stream in Alaska tangled with a porky on at least three different occasions during the same summer. Every time, the bear got a face full of quills for its efforts. Even her three young cubs wandered around with quills stuck in their noses.

After the third time, the mother bear didn't recover as quickly as she had before. She began to lose weight and grow weak. Moving slowly, as if her front paws were painful to walk on, she caught very few salmon when she came to fish. Most of the time, she just ate the scraps left by other bears. When this female was last spotted in late autumn, she was much thinner than bears normally are at that time of the year. When a mother bear fails to gain weight before she dens for the winter, she may be unable to produce enough milk to feed her cubs, and they could starve to death.

While caribou and elk usually offer no help when their calves are being chased by a bear, the mother moose whose young are threatened is a fighter. A photographer friend of mine watched a grizzly try to snatch a young moose calf from beside its mother. The female charged the bear, lashing out with the sharp hooves on her front

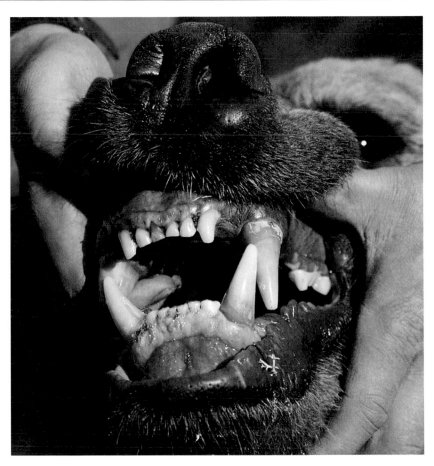

feet. The bear limped away, leaving the mother and her calf in peace.

In another incident, a black bear grabbed a moose calf as the calf called out to its mother. The female moose raced toward the calf and jumped on the bear's back with her heavy hooves,

cutting a deep gash across the bear's shoulder. The bear immediately released the calf, and it escaped.

Bears are large, intimidating animals with dangerous equipment in their mouths and paws. Just the same, they don't always get their way.

The Enemies of Bears

What is the most common enemy of bears? Is it mountain lions? Wolves? Tigers? The truth is that although all these animals attack bears, the most common enemy of bears is other bears. They sometimes even kill and eat each other.

In most scenarios, it's dangerous for one bear to attack another. A bear is skilled at defending itself, and an attacking bear can suffer serious injuries. This high risk tends to discourage a bear from attacking another, except when that bear has something to gain. Here's an example of just such an incident.

One October, in northern Hudson Bay, a large male polar bear was seen in the vicinity of a female. So thin that his bony hips and shoulders showed through his sagging skin, the male nevertheless successfully attacked and killed the female and then ate her.

Nearby, a 2-year-old cub watched nervously. The dead bear was probably its mother. In all likelihood, the attack occurred because the male was starving. Perhaps the male bear had tried to attack the young bear first, and the mother had been killed defending her cub. Mother bears often exhibit a strong instinct to protect their young.

Safely tucked away in its winter den, a hibernating bear, one might imagine, is free from danger. Not so. Large adult male bears have been known to attack smaller, weaker bears as they lie curled up inside their dens. In such situations, it is almost impossible for a bear to escape a surprise attack.

Although there are many stories about bears killing each other, it is still a fairly rare event in their everyday lives. We should remember, however, that when one bear kills another bear, it is neither right nor wrong. It is simply a bear acting in the only way it knows how to act—like a bear.

Bear Facts

In the water, a polar bear may be attacked and killed by a bull walrus.

—

Black bears are most vulnerable to attack by wolves when trapped inside their winter dens.

—

A brown bear may attack and kill a black bear, which explains why a black bear rarely strays far from large trees it can shinny up to escape.

—

In the arenas of ancient Rome, brown bears and lions were forced to fight each other to the death.

Tigers, Wolves and Bears

Tigers are aggressive predators, and in Russia, tigers hunt bears. Russian tigers, which weigh up to 300 kilograms (660 lb), are larger than most Asiatic black bears. They are even bigger than most brown bears that inhabit the same regions the tigers do. Bear-hunting season for the tiger typically starts when the bears have settled into their winter dens. It's difficult for a cornered bear to defend itself in a small, cramped place with only one exit. Fear of tigers is one reason that Asiatic black bears often den in tree cavities high off the ground, where a tiger can't easily reach them.

Brown bears, on the other hand, are not good tree climbers and must therefore den on the ground, and that's just where the tigers find them. There are many stories of Russian tigers killing brown bears and eating them. In one, a hungry tiger located a mother brown bear and her two cubs denned together in a hole under the roots of a tree. The entrance to the den was small, so at first, the mother bear was able to keep the tiger at bay. But when the tiger moved to the rear of the den and began to dig out the bear family, the frightened mother was flushed

A brown bear rears up on its hind legs to see other bears better. Cubs and juveniles typically stand up when they are intimidated by the larger bears. Adult female bears, such as this one, rarely stand upright.

When tuckered out from a long journey or when threatened by a predator, a polar bear cub may clamber onto its mother's back.

from the den. The tiger then grabbed her by the back of the neck, killing her instantly, and proceeded to kill the two cubs in the usual tiger fashion, with a bite to the throat.

While there are no tigers in North America, there is another predator that poses a significant threat to denning bears: wolves. Smaller than bears, wolves do their best work in packs, and a lone bear is often no match for a pack of wolves.

In Minnesota, nine wolves surrounded and killed a denning mother black bear and her cubs. The same thing happened when a pack of eight wolves found a black bear denning in Alberta. It's one thing for wolves to attack a black bear, but do they ever tackle the more powerful bears? I learned firsthand about the hunting skills of a pack of wolves that ambushed a mother polar bear along the coast of Hudson Bay.

The mother bear and her two newborn cubs had just left their winter den. The bears were heading down a frozen stream when four wolves intercepted the family. The wolves surrounded the mother, and while she was distracted, one of them grabbed a cub and ran off with it. The wolves then abandoned the mother bear, and she escaped with the remaining cub running close behind her. But once the wolves had killed and eaten the first cub, they picked up the trail of the mother polar bear and soon caught up with her. Again, there were too many wolves for the mother bear to protect her cub successfully. The wolves easily caught and killed the second cub.

Bugging a Bear

Every summer, I travel to the Arctic to take photographs, and every summer, I get bugged by the bugs. As soon as the temperature rises, bloodsucking insects swarm over every animal that breathes in the Arctic, and that includes bears as well as photographers.

In the Yukon and Alaska, mosquitoes zero in on the brown bear, targeting the sensitive skin on the bear's nose and lips and around its eyes. The worst month is July. Every time a bear slows down to nibble on some plants, a dense cloud of mosquitoes forms around it, and the bear has no choice but to move along or else be bitten relentlessly. Sometimes a bear gets so bugged that it races across the tundra, shaking its head in frustration, frantically trying to outrun the mosquitoes. But the mosquitoes follow. At times like these, a bear searches out one of the few remaining patches

Like every warm-blooded animal in the North, brown bears are attacked by swarms of bloodsucking mosquitoes for several weeks during the warmest days of the short Arctic summer. Bears have little defense against these pests but to hide in dens or to escape onto snow patches.

of snow, where it is able to rest and enjoy a temporary respite from the biting swarms.

The black bear dodges mosquitoes by climbing high into a tree, where the breezes blow the insects away. When the bugs get really pesky, the bear may even return to its winter den and hide inside.

Mosquito-bugged polar bears along the western coast of Hudson Bay dig out earth dens to escape from the insect pests. The mosquitoes in that area can be so bad, it's impossible to breathe without inhaling a mouthful. The bears dig the dens so deep that they reach permanently frozen ground. The tunnels leading to the dens may be up to six meters (20 ft) long. At the bottom of the tunnels, the dens are dark, cool and mercifully bug-free.

A Bunch of Bears

We already know that a bear spends much of its life alone. That can change, though, when there is enough food in one area to feed many bears at a time. Along one stretch of Alaska's McNeil River that was no longer than a football field, 109 brown bears spent a July day fishing for salmon together. In another sighting, 56 polar bears gathered around a dead bowhead whale floating in the Arctic pack ice and shared a 55-tonne (60 ton) meal of blubber and meat. As many as eight adult polar bears fed shoulder to shoulder. American black bears also congregate in groups to feast on large blueberry patches or when nosing around at dumpsites for something to eat.

Whenever bears come together in a bunch like this, they need some way to keep the peace. Bears do this by establishing a pecking order, or hierarchy, in which there are top-ranking animals, middle-ranking animals and those at the bottom. In the bear world, the largest and strongest bears—the adult males—are usually at the top of the hierarchy. Next are adult females with cubs, then solitary females, followed by the 2-to-4-year-olds, which I call teenage bears. Cubs, being the smallest, are naturally at the bottom of the hierarchy.

How does a hierarchy work? Pretend you're a brown bear fishing for salmon, and your rank among the bears around you is somewhere in the middle. Suddenly, a big top-ranking male bear comes out of the bushes and wants your fishing spot or, even worse, the fat salmon you just pulled from the water. What do you do? Simple. You give him what he wants. You may roar and protest, but nevertheless, you back away and leave the fish.

Then what do you do? If you're still hungry, you move along the edge of the stream until you meet a bear that has both a good fishing spot and a lower rank than you. You drop your head and flatten your ears to let the bear know you mean business, and then you steal its fishing spot. The

Bear Facts

Black bears can run at speeds of up to 40 kilometers per hour (25 mph).

—

Bears sometimes form alliances with each other to improve their status in the local hierarchy.

—

Bears rely on visual, vocal and odor signals to communicate with each other.

loser must now find a bear that *it* can push around.

From the time it is a cub, a bear learns how to figure out where it fits in the hierarchy and how to recognize the rank of other bears. Generally, big bears bully small bears and old bears bully young bears. The result of all this bullying is that many bears can live close together without fighting too much and injuring each other. Basically, disagreements are settled by a simple decision about which bear has the higher rank.

It is not always this straightforward. Sometimes a low-ranking bear can get what it wants despite its position near the bottom of the hierarchy. Suppose a very hungry teenage bear with a low rank spots an adult female that has just caught a juicy salmon. The teenager may try to steal the fish, and surprisingly, it sometimes succeeds. The female may let the younger bear have the fish because, at that particular moment, she's not very hungry and doesn't want to argue over the salmon. Besides, if she really wants to nibble on a salmon, she can catch another one.

A low-ranking teenage bear has another way of getting what it wants: it can join forces with one or two other teenage bears. A "gang" is able to get its members more to eat.

All bears communicate using body posture, head and ear position and vocalizations. These brown bears are wrangling over a prized fishing spot in a salmon stream. The bear on the right won the argument.

Teenage Bears

A teenage bear is a young bear that has left its mother but is not yet old enough to mate. In the bear world, most young bears are teenagers for two to three years, and these are usually the most difficult years of a bear's life. A young bear can no longer run to its mother for protection from other bears. Instead, it must search for its own food and dig its own winter den. And when it finds a good meal, a higher-ranking bear often comes along and steals it.

Bears move around a lot during the teenage years, looking for a place to fit in and trying to stay out of trouble with other bears. Eventually, most of them learn what they need to know and settle into a familiar home range.

Young female black bears, like many female bears, are little homebodies that stay close to their mother's home range and do not stray far from the place they were born. In fact, they often either inherit part of their mother's home range or move to an area nearby.

Male teenage bears are exactly the opposite. Apparently programmed to wander far from home, young American black bears may travel more than 200 kilometers (125 mi) from their mother's home range before they finally settle down. Young brown bears often travel twice that distance,

and some young polar bears make journeys of more than 1,000 kilometers (600 mi). Most young males probably never see their mother again once they leave her range, whereas young female bears may bump into their mother over and over again throughout their lives.

When male teenage bears travel such long distances, they move through completely foreign territory. Often, they face trouble when they encounter the resident bears. Sometimes they even get into fights and are injured. I once examined a young brown bear that had been killed when it fell from

---

Bear Facts

Most bear families break up at the beginning of the spring breeding season.

—

Young black bears stay with their mothers until they are 1½ years old, whereas young brown bears and polar bears usually remain until they are about 3.

—

Newly independent male bears often get into trouble with people when they wander into towns and raid garbage cans.

---

a cliff. The dead bear had several deep tooth marks on its face and a fresh cut on the side of its neck. I guessed that the teenage bear had been attacked by a larger bear, and in its haste to escape, it had accidentally tumbled off the cliff.

Young male bears have a rough time fitting into the bear world, and as a result, they occasionally find the living easier in the human world. The young black bears that have wandered into cities and towns and attracted the attention of the local news media are frequently teenage males that have recently left home and are on a cross-country trip. These inexperienced bears have difficulty finding enough food to eat and sometimes resort to raiding garbage cans. Pretty soon, they become a nuisance.

Usually, these problem teenage bears are livetrapped and moved back to the wilderness, away from people. If they are not transported far enough away, however, they often return to the scene of the crime two or three days later. Repeat offenders are either shot or, worse, sentenced to life imprisonment in a zoo.

Leaving Home
Young black bears usually leave home in their second summer, when they are 1½ years old. Young brown bears

Because juvenile bears have a low position in the hierarchy, they are often forced to forage for food in the poorest areas. Even so, this young polar bear is quite fat, a testament to its hunting skills.

The first few years after a brown bear leaves its mother and her home range are some of the most difficult in its life. The inexperienced "teenager" is bullied and pushed around by older and larger bears.

and polar bears stay with their families longer, separating from their mothers when they are 2½, sometimes 3½ years old. When it's time for the family to break up, a cub may stray farther and farther from its mother, gradually spending more time alone. Eventually, the two drift apart for good. Sometimes the breakup is a little more dramatic.

At the McNeil River State Game Sanctuary one year, a mother brown bear's behavior toward her cubs literally changed overnight. One morning, she was suddenly very aggressive toward her two cubs. She charged them over and over again, biting and swatting the cubs several times in an effort to drive them away. The next day, the family split up. In the days that followed, the mother bear mated with three different male bears.

It was June, and June is the mating season, the time when most bear families separate. Only at this time of year does a mother bear no longer run away when male bears come sniffing around. The cubs are understandably frightened by the large males, and they keep their distance from their mother. When the mating season is over, the mother and her cubs are almost never reunited, although on rare occasions, they do get back together for the remainder of the summer.

A trio of juvenile brown bears wanders across a tidal flat in search of food. Sometimes these teenage "gangs" are littermates that remain together after leaving their mother. They can also be unrelated bears of the same age that have temporarily joined forces for security.

Winter Hideaways

I remember how nervous I was the first time I approached a bear's den. The den, which was at the base of a tree, housed a mother black bear and her two cubs. As I drew nearer, I could feel my heart hammering against my rib cage. Mother bears are famous for exercising their protective instincts, and I was sure the bear was going to charge out at any moment, snarling and drooling, and tear me to pieces. Naively, I stood near a tree that I could climb if I suddenly needed to escape. What I didn't know then was that if the bear had wanted to, she could have climbed the tree and been waiting for me at the top.

On this field trip, I was with a biologist friend who planned to tranquilize the bears in order to examine them. My friend crept up to the mouth of the den and shone a flashlight inside to check the mother bear's position. With the light still shining on the mother, he aimed his dart pistol and fired a shot into her shoulder. What would she do next? Luckily, the mother bear stayed huddled inside the den, curled around her cubs. The tranquilizer dart quickly took effect and put her into a drugged sleep.

Bears hibernate for the same reasons that other northern animals do—to avoid a time of the year when food is scarce and the weather conditions are severe. A hibernating animal bunks down for the winter simply to conserve energy. Of the planet's eight species of bears, only the four northern bears, which have in common a sometimes unfriendly climate, hibernate.

How long a bear hibernates depends on where it lives. Let's consider the American black bear, which ranges from the Arctic regions of Alaska to the subtropical forests of Florida. In Alaska, where the winters are long and severe, a black bear may hibernate for eight months of the year. As we move south, bears generally hibernate for shorter periods. In Alberta, a black bear may den for six months, whereas in Virginia, it may

---

Bear Facts

The largest polar bear denning area in North America is near Churchill, Manitoba, where 150 to 200 polar bears den each winter.

—

Only the four species of northern bears den in the winter.

—

One pregnant black bear in Alaska spent a record 247 days in her winter den.

---

hibernate for just four months. In Florida, where the winters are mild, a black bear may not hibernate at all.

Bears choose a variety of places in which to hibernate. I have seen bears den in brush piles, at the base of uprooted trees and under fallen logs. Asiatic and American black bears often den in cavities at the top of large trees, sometimes 21 meters (70 ft) off the ground. In a survey conducted in Tennessee, the average opening to a tree cavity was found to be only 30 by 55 centimeters (12 x 22 in). Imagine weighing 150 kilograms (330 lb) and trying to squeeze through such a small hole. But the bears do it.

In cartoons, bears are frequently shown living inside huge caves, but in reality, their dens are rarely that big. I have crawled into many rock dens. Most of them had two or three different entrances, and some had multiple chambers. The larger dens are often used by a mother and her cubs, with each animal curling up in its own little space.

The chamber in most dens has just enough space for a bear to squirm around in but never enough room for it to stand up. I am over six feet tall and have crawled inside many dens (always when the bear wasn't home). Usually, there was just enough room for me to lie on my side, curled up.

Polar bears dig their winter dens in snowdrifts. The tunnel of this den was 2.5 meters (8 ft) long and led to an egg-shaped chamber 2 meters (6½ ft) in diameter.

When dens are small like this, a hibernating bear's body temperature is able to heat the den much more efficiently. As a result, not only does the animal burn fewer calories trying to stay warm, but it uses less of its fat reserves than if it were struggling to heat a much larger den. A biologist friend of mine, Dr. Gary Alt, compared the size of an average black bear den with that of an average human bedroom. From his calculations, Alt determined that 62 black bears in hibernation mode would fit inside a bedroom. Can you imagine how hot and stuffy that would get—especially if you were the one sleeping on the bottom?

One of the most unusual places for a bear to spend the winter is in a surface nest. Some black bears in the eastern United States chew off branches and build a nest on the ground, just as some birds do. One nest I examined had been used by a mother black bear and her two cubs. The mother had bitten off hundreds of branches, 30 to 60 centimeters (12-24 in) in length, and constructed a thick nest that she lined with dried grasses and leaves. In many ways, the nest was like a fancy day bed. Another bear built a nest on top of an old muskrat house in the middle of a marsh, while still another bedded down on a beaver dam.

In North America, the most common place for a black bear or a brown bear to hibernate for the winter is in a simple hole in the ground, dug by the bear itself. Most of the holes, called excavation dens, collapse in the spring after the bear leaves, so a new den must be dug each autumn. Bears have learned that an ideal location for an excavation den is at the base of a tree or a clump of bushes, where the roots act as a built-in support so that the den roof doesn't collapse. Bushes and tree roots also help to trap snow and prevent it from blowing away, providing a thick layer of snowy insulation that covers the entrance to the den and keeps it warmer.

Most excavation dens have a one to two-meter-long (3-6½ ft) tunnel leading to a single egg-shaped chamber. There was one den in Alaska, however, where a brown bear had just kept digging and digging and digging. When the bear had finally run out of steam, it had dug a tunnel 6.5 meters (21 ft) long!

A bear frequently lines its den with material it finds nearby, since dried vegetation helps to insulate the bear from the cold ground. Using its claws to drag leaves, needles and grasses inside the den, the bear builds a thick, cozy mattress up to 45 centimeters (18 in) deep. I have seen many black bear dens that looked as though someone had raked the area around the mouth of the den for a good 30 square meters (36 sq yd).

One energetic black bear in Michigan stole hay from a stack in a farmer's field and carried it over 100 meters (325 ft) into a nearby swamp to use as bedding in its winter den. Even bears that den in tree cavities will scrape wood shavings from the inside of the tree to line the bottom of the den.

If a denning spot looks good, a bear may settle into some unusual places. In Pennsylvania, a black bear denned inside a tree right beside a family's driveway. Every time the owner of the house got in and out of his car, he walked within three meters (10 ft) of the sleeping bear. The man had no idea who was spending the winter as his neighbor.

Taking advantage of structures that are already intact, bears frequently den under cottages and camps built in the woods. I crawled under one such structure and discovered that the bear had chewed halfway through the beam supporting the floor and used the wood chips to line the den. Likewise, biologist Alt followed the signal from the radio-collar on a large black bear and found the animal denning under a hunting cabin. It just so happened that a group of noisy bear hunters was inside at the time, and they asked Alt where they could get themselves a bear. Alt just shrugged his shoulders. The hunters never did stumble on the black bear curled up right under their feet and had to return to the city empty-handed.

Dens in the Snow

Most of the northern bears live in areas where winter lasts six months or more each year and where snow piles up in deep, insulating drifts. Surprisingly, neither brown bears nor either species of black bear (American and Asiatic) dig their dens in the snow. The polar bear, on the other hand, always dens in the snow.

The architecture of a polar bear's snow den is similar to that of an earth den, except it is excavated from the snow. A tunnel several meters long leads to an oval chamber two to three meters (6½-10 ft) in diameter and about a meter or so (3-4 ft) high.

The roof on some snow dens may be three meters (10 ft) thick. Loosely packed snow is a good insulator, so the temperature inside a polar bear's den is usually much higher than the temperature on the outside. One winter, an enthusiastic biologist named Dr. Paul Watts threaded a temperature probe through the ceiling of a polar

When members of a polar bear family first emerge from their winter den, they may spend several weeks in the area. During this time, the mother bear recovers from the drowsiness of hibernation and her cubs exercise, gain strength and become acclimatized to the outside cold.

bear den so that he could monitor the inside temperature. Over the course of the month-long study, the temperature inside the den was never more than two or three degrees below freezing, even though the outside temperature dropped as low as minus 30 degrees C (–22°F). At times, the den was 33 Celsius degrees (60F°) warmer than the outside air.

Just as remarkable is the fact that Watts was brave enough to poke a hole through the roof of an occupied polar bear den in the first place. I always meant to ask him what he had planned to do if the ceiling of the den had suddenly collapsed. I guess the best he could have hoped for was to be quickly adopted.

When it comes to denning, polar bears are very different from the other

Here, a polar bear cub is inside the winter den where it was born. The mother bear's claw marks are clearly visible in the walls of the den. The sunlight is coming through a hole in the roof dug by the mother.

northern bears. Meat-eating polar bears can continue to hunt seals throughout most of the winter, so they don't need to retreat to a den to conserve energy, as the largely vegetarian brown bears and black bears must do. Because of this, only pregnant female polar bears spend any significant amounts of time in a den during the winter, usually four or five months. The den provides the mother polar bear with a warm, protected environment where she can give birth to her cubs. As soon as the cubs are 3 months old and big enough to travel, the mother polar bear and her offspring leave the den to start hunting.

Hungry as a Bear

In late summer and early autumn, bears prepare for the months of winter denning by eating, eating, eating. A bear may spend 20 hours a day feeding on berries, nuts, acorns or salmon. At this time of the year, it has an appetite that just won't quit. As a result, a bear will consume up to 20,000 calories a day, three to four times its normal intake. For you or me, that would be the same thing as eating 43 hamburgers and 12 large orders of French fries—every day.

All this eating leads to one thing: obesity. It's fortunate, then, that an obese bear is a happy bear. In autumn, the typical brown bear puts on up to 1.5 kilograms (3 lb) every day. One young grizzly from Yellowstone National Park gained 20 kilograms (45 lb) in just 12 days, and an adult male brown bear from Alaska increased its weight by over 90 kilograms (200 lb) in two months. Black bears also have a reputation for packing on the pounds. In Pennsylvania, a 10-year-old male gained 58 kilograms (128 lb) from late summer to mid-September.

Why do bears suddenly stuff themselves silly? In hibernation, a bear won't eat or drink anything. Remember, a black bear in Alaska may hibernate for seven to eight months. During that time, the bear must rely totally on its fat reserves to fuel it through the long, dark days of winter, when it will lose an average 25 to 30 percent of its body weight. After a bear comes out of hibernation in the spring, there is usually very little food available. Most bears continue to lose weight until June or even mid-July, as they burn up the last of their fat supplies. So the yearly cycle of a typical bear is half a year of eating, followed by half a year of starving. Feast and famine, feast and famine.

Baby Bears

Most animals that make their home in the North give birth to their young in the spring, once the warm temperatures have returned. Not so for northern bears. Mother bears have their babies during the coldest, darkest months of the winter. As a result, polar bear cubs are usually born in late November or early December, and black bear and brown bear cubs are born in January or February.

The size of a bear family is heavily influenced by one factor: the mother bear's diet. Female bears living where there is an abundant food supply throughout the summer and autumn before their cubs are born have larger litters than females living in habitats where food is scarce or poor in quality. The best example of this is found among American black bears. Let's compare the black bears in two different U.S. locations: Pennsylvania and Montana.

Pennsylvania black bears enjoy a rich diet of beechnuts, acorns, wild cherries and grapes; as a consequence, female black bears in Pennsylvania commonly have litters of three or four cubs. Not only do Pennsylvania bears have large litters, but they also raise a new litter of cubs every two years.

Now consider the black bears in Montana. As a result of this state's cold, harsh winters and hot, dry sum-mers, the bears have a meager food supply and the females therefore produce fewer cubs. Black bears in Montana normally have only one or two cubs per litter and may produce a litter just once every three or four years.

Another way to illustrate the difference between the black bears in these two regions is to compare the number of cubs a typical mother bear has in her lifetime. In Montana, a female black bear will produce, on average, nine cubs during her lifetime; a female in Pennsylvania, on the other hand, will typically give birth to 28 cubs!

Diet also influences the number of cubs a female brown bear will produce. Brown bears living along the coast of Alaska can feast on energy-rich salmon each summer. These well-fed females have more cubs than do females that live in the northern Yukon, where bears must survive on a skimpy diet of roots and berries.

Female polar bears have the same diet everywhere they live, so unlike brown bears and black bears, female polar bears produce the same number of cubs no matter where they live in the Arctic. Most have litters of one or two cubs, although they may, on rare occasions, produce triplets.

Among the tropical bears—the sun bear, spectacled bear, giant panda and sloth bear—litter size is likewise limited to one or two cubs. Although none of these bears are forced to hibernate as a defense against bad weather and a drastically reduced food supply, they do not have the luxury of the rich diet enjoyed by some northern black and brown bears. For the tropical bears, the daily search for food is an ongoing struggle.

Screamers and Hummers
There is only one word to describe a newborn bear cub, and that word is ugly. At birth, a bear cub is surprisingly small—about the size of a chubby chipmunk. It is toothless, its eyelids are sealed shut, and its ears are just fleshy tabs on the sides of its head. Almost naked-looking, the cub

Bear Facts

When bear cubs suckle, they make a loud humming noise, known as a nursing chuckle.

—

As a female black bear ages, she has more cubs in each litter.

—

Polar bears produce the richest milk of any bear: with 47 percent fat, it is thicker than whipping cream.

These 3-month-old polar bear cubs have just left the family's winter den and moved onto the sea ice. They will just drink milk until they are 4 or 5 months of age.

A rare photograph of a newborn black bear cub illustrates how small and helpless these animals are. Despite having a mother that weighs more than 136 kilograms (300 lb), this cub is only 23 centimeters (9 in) long and weighs a mere 360 grams (12½ oz).

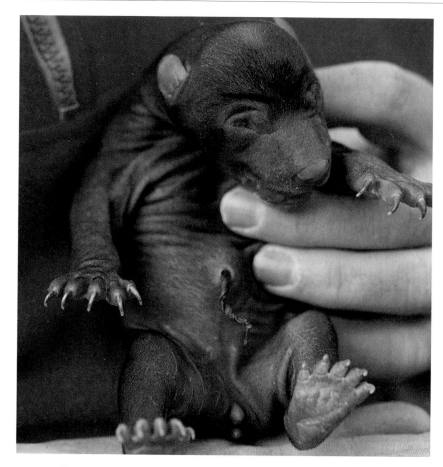

is actually covered with fine, short hair. What cubs lack in looks, however, they make up for in voice; these little bears are screamers.

A bear cub screams loudly whenever it is hungry, cold or frightened. That is probably a good thing, because the cub's mother is hibernating when the cub is born, and she may be drowsy and slow to react. The sound of a high-pitched squeal quickly alerts the mother that the cub needs her help.

Bear cubs are just as noisy when they are nursing. All northern bear cubs produce a continuous humming sound the whole time they are suckling. The noise is so loud that I have heard it while standing outside the winter den of a black bear family. No other baby carnivore hums in this way; I believe it evolved in bears so that cubs could signal to their sleepy mother that she should release her milk and not move around too much.

Milk is the miracle food that provides young animals with all the nutrients they need to grow, and bears are no exception. In fact, bear milk is richer than the milk of most animals. Everyone has tasted the difference between whole and skim milk from a cow. Whole milk contains about 4 percent fat, while skim milk is simply cow's milk that has had most of the fat removed. Imagine how creamy bear milk would taste, since it often contains 25 to 30 percent fat. The milk of some polar bears contains a whopping 47 percent fat. That's thicker than whipping cream!

Naturally, newborn cubs grow very quickly on a diet of such rich, fatty milk. By the time a mother bear is ready to abandon her winter den in the spring, the cubs have grown into sizable little bears. At this time, young black bear cubs weigh between 3 and 4 kilograms (6-9 lb), young polar bears weigh between 9 and 11 kilo-

Photograph by Gary Alt

American black bear cubs have blue-gray eyes when they are born. The eyes gradually become dark brown when the young bears are between 6 and 8 months old.

grams (20-25 lb) and young brown bears weigh something in between. Bear cubs at this age are no longer homely, wrinkled little critters but have grown into beautiful balls of fur that are filled with energy and are a delight to watch and photograph.

The time a newborn bear spends with its mother in the winter den is probably the least dangerous time of a cub's life. Once the family leaves the den in spring, many bear cubs die. Most of them die of starvation or from diseases, but some are killed by other bears or predators such as wolves, coyotes, mountain lions and bobcats. In fact, one-quarter to one-half of all bear cubs do not live to see their first birthday. Life for a bear of any age is never easy, but it is particularly difficult for cubs.

People and Bears

For thousands of years, bears have played an important role in the lives of Arctic and northern peoples, and as a result, bears are featured in many of the elaborate customs and ceremonies that emerged from these cultures. Most of the customs involved the hunting of bears, the handling of the dead animals and the disposal of their bones. The ceremonies took different forms in Russia, Japan, Norway and North America, but the common theme was an attitude of respect and reverence for the animal. I wrote about these ancient customs in *Bears: Monarchs of the Northern Wilderness* (GreyStone Books, Douglas & McIntyre; 1993):

"Bears were most often hunted while the animals were in their winter dens. They were driven from their dens, sometimes with fire, and killed as they attempted to escape. Many times, a hunter, clad only in skins, would engage the bear in hand-to-claw combat as the aroused animal rushed from its refuge....

"Before a hunt, or while the men surrounded the bear, one of the hunters would deliver a speech to the animal, explaining why the men were about to kill it, perhaps saying that they needed to feed their hungry children or to clothe themselves against the fury of winter. The spokesman would then apologize to the bear for the act the men were about to commit and beg the bear not to seek revenge on them in the afterlife....

"After the bear was [stabbed with] a spear or [beaten to death] with an axe, the dead animal continued to be handled in a ceremonial fashion so as not to offend its spirit. Onlookers never pointed at the bear, and they never addressed the animal directly. When people spoke about the dead bear, they used [expressions] of respect.... They called the bear grandfather or 'old man with the fur garment.' Taboos were associated with different parts of the bear's body. For example, in some cultures, the head

Bear Facts

Hunting by humans is the leading cause of death in adult bears of all species.

—

A fascination with bears has been part of human culture since the Stone Age.

—

Bloody fights between bulls and bears were a common spectator "sport" in the early days of California.

and paws of a bear could not be eaten or even handled by women, and only men could eat the rump meat.

"Additional customs dictated how a bear's remains were to be treated. Particular care was taken in disposing of the skull. Often, it was placed in a tree in the forest or mounted on a special pole, sometimes at the site where the bear was killed. The bear's other bones were treated with equal [care]. Most often, they were buried or wrapped in bark and hung in a tree along with the skull. It was an evil omen if the bear's bones happened to get chewed on by a hunter's dogs."

Ancient hunters believed that all animals had a spirit, or soul, and that the spirit of a dead animal could bring good or bad luck to the hunter, depending on how the hunter behaved and treated the animal after it was dead. To them, the bear was an equal. This attitude changed dramatically when people became farmers and herders of cattle and sheep.

Suddenly, the bear was our enemy, and we waged war against it. We chased bears with killer dogs, we hunted and shot them for sport and revenge, we poisoned them, and we trapped and imprisoned them in cramped little cages. Even then, people were not content. They wanted to do more than destroy bears; they

The town of Churchill, Manitoba, calls itself "The Polar Bear Capital of the World." More than 5,000 visitors travel to the region every autumn to watch polar bears.

wanted to control and torture them. One of the worst examples of this urge is the bear and bull fights that were held in California in the mid-1800s.

Bear and bull fights always attracted large crowds of bloodthirsty spectators. First, a bear was dragged into the arena, then a thick leather rope, 20 meters (65 ft) long, was tied to its hind leg. The other end of the rope was strapped to the front leg of a wild bull. The bull and the bear were then prodded to fight each other. If the animals were reluctant to battle, they were jabbed with a nail fixed to the end of a stick. The animals had no choice but to fight for their lives.

The spectators cheered in unison as the bull charged and smashed its horns against the bear's ribs, knocking the bear onto its back. When the

Biologist Larry Aumiller has been the manager of Alaska's McNeil River State Game Sanctuary since 1976. The brown bears in the sanctuary are very accustomed to people, and the bears are given the right-of-way. No one has been seriously injured by a bear in the sanctuary in almost 20 years—proof that bears and people can live together.

enraged bear grabbed the bull's nose in its powerful jaws, the bull bellowed in pain and struggled desperately to free itself. Dust and blood filled the arena, and the crowd cheered even louder. After the first bull was killed, another was led in, and the battered bear was forced to fight again for its life. Often, the exhausted bear fought three or four bulls in succession, until it was finally gored to death.

Our attitude toward bears today is vastly different than that of a century ago. Every year, hundreds of thousands of people flock to our national parks, most of them hoping to catch a glimpse of a bear. Bear viewing has become so popular that people now take special vacations just to observe bears. People travel to China to watch giant pandas chewing on bamboo, they journey to Alaska to view brown bears fishing for salmon, they set off on elephants in Nepal to search for sloth bears, and they sail along the coast of British Columbia hoping to see a white spirit bear.

Every October for more than 12 years, I have guided small groups of tourists to Churchill, Manitoba, to observe polar bears along the western coast of Hudson Bay. In that time, I have watched hundreds of people view a polar bear for the first time, and I know what an impact these

animals can have on them: Even the most hardened city dweller rallies to the cause of the polar bear and its wilderness world.

On one such tour, we watched a mother bear and her cub roll and wrestle in a snowdrift for almost an hour. Afterward, everyone was giddy from the excitement of the experience, and one woman from New York City expressed the feelings of everyone in the group when she said: "These magnificent animals should never be allowed to disappear."

The Future of Bears

Bears first appeared on Earth 15 million to 20 million years ago, long after the dinosaurs had disappeared. Since then, dozens of different species of bears have emerged, survived for a time, then faded and become extinct in the slow process of evolution. The most recent wave of bear extinctions occurred at the end of the last Ice Age, just 10,000 to 15,000 years ago.

The bears which disappeared at that time were the short-faced bears, a tribe of bears that included the giant short-faced bear of North America, possibly the largest bear ever to walk on the face of our planet. The giant short-faced bear was a meat-eating predator that, on all fours, stood as tall as a man and ran down its prey in the same way lions and tigers do today. The spectacled bear of South America is the only surviving descendant of the short-faced bear tribe.

As we learned earlier, there are just eight species of bears alive in the world today. Unfortunately, the populations of only two of those species—the polar bear and the American black bear—are not declining.

Currently, the world polar bear population is stable at around 30,000 to 40,000 individuals. For the past 30 years, the five polar nations (Greenland, Canada, United States, Norway and Russia) have held regular meetings and freely shared scientific information. As a consequence, international measures have been taken to ensure that these magnificent bears will survive into the future. The polar bear's survival is one of the great conservation success stories of this century and is a testament to the power of global cooperation.

The population of the American black bear, which numbers around 400,000 animals, is the largest bear population in the world. In fact, there are more American black bears than there are of the seven other species of bears combined. It is possibly the

---

Bear Facts

*American black bears
are found in 32 U.S. states,
5 Mexican states and every
province in Canada except
Prince Edward Island.*

—

*Of the eight species of bears
worldwide, only the polar bear
and American black bear
populations are not in decline.*

—

*Seeing a bear in the wild is the
number-one wildlife wish among
visitors to North American parks.*

---

most flexible and adaptable of all the bears, and its ability to live in a great variety of habitats, from deserts to forests and tundra, has allowed the American black bear to flourish.

Unfortunately, the story for the remaining bear species is not as encouraging: all six species are slowly disappearing. Of these, the brown bear is probably in the best shape.

Biologists estimate that there are 40,000 to 50,000 brown bears still thriving in North America. These are distributed more or less equally between Alaska and western Canada, with a small population of 800 to 1,000 brown bears still hanging on in Glacier and Yellowstone National Parks, in Montana and Wyoming. The brown bear also makes its home in Europe and Asia, but we don't know how many bears live there. In the 1980s, there were 100,000 brown bears in Russia alone, but today, there are far fewer than that, possibly fewer than there are in North America, and these bears are vanishing rapidly.

Bears are difficult animals to count. Generally, they are secretive, they occur in low numbers spread over large areas, and they are often nocturnal. Because of this, no one knows exactly how many Asiatic black bears, sun bears, sloth bears or spectacled bears remain in the wild. Biologists know

Getting close to a family of brown bears such as this would not be safe, or even possible, in most areas of the world. This family lives in Alaska's McNeil River State Game Sanctuary, where the protected bears have become completely comfortable with the presence of humans.

that these bears are disappearing, but they don't know how fast their populations are declining.

The giant panda of China is the bear that is most threatened with extinction. Biologists estimate that there are fewer than 1,000 giant pandas alive today in the wild, and the prospects for the future are not good.

Why are so many species of bears in decline? As with the giant panda in China, the number-one reason for the decline of bear populations is the uncontrolled growth of the human population. Currently, the world's population is soaring toward six billion people, and every week, two million more must squeeze onto our planet. People need space to live and to grow food, and the more there are of us, the less space there is for bears and other wildlife. It is not surprising, then, that the wilderness home of bears everywhere is being rapidly gobbled up by people. Even most of the areas that have been spared will soon be completely surrounded by humans. As people and bears move closer and closer together, other problems arise. Bears often like the same foods that we do, and when they raid a farmer's crops, they are shot, trapped or poisoned.

The future of bears, however, is not quite as bleak as it sounds. Consider the story of the polar bear. In the 1950s, polar bears were slowly being eliminated; the world population was thought to be less than 15,000. Now, after only three decades of conservation and management, the polar bear numbers 30,000 to 40,000 and is one of the few species of bears not in decline. The question is not whether bears can survive with people but whether people can survive with bears. Humans must decide whether it is important to have bears in the world, and everyone, including you, has a voice in this decision.

Today, there are many conservation groups fighting for the rights of bears and other wildlife. By joining organizations such as the World Wildlife Fund, the Nature Conservancy of Canada and the Sierra Club, you can help make a difference.

Worldwide Distribution

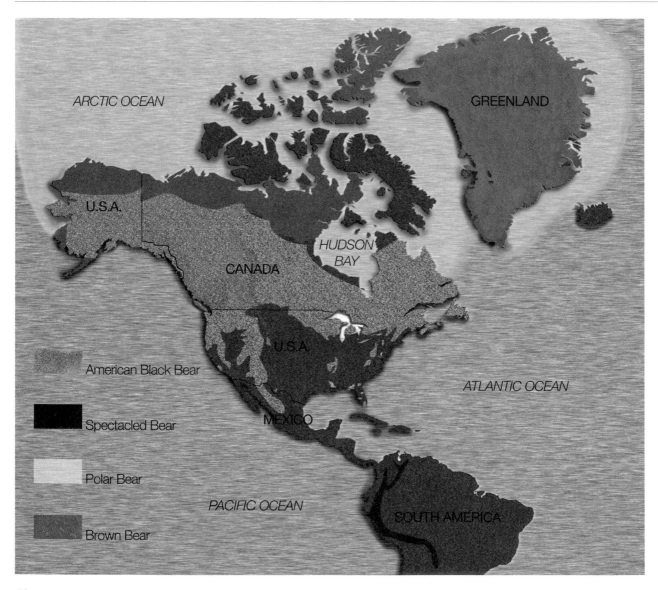

ARCTIC OCEAN

GREENLAND

U.S.A.

CANADA

HUDSON BAY

American Black Bear

Spectacled Bear

Polar Bear

Brown Bear

U.S.A.

ATLANTIC OCEAN

MEXICO

PACIFIC OCEAN

SOUTH AMERICA

Please note the change in color where ranges overlap: The American black bear's range overlaps the brown bear's; the Asiatic black bear's overlaps those of the sun bear, the sloth bear and the brown bear.

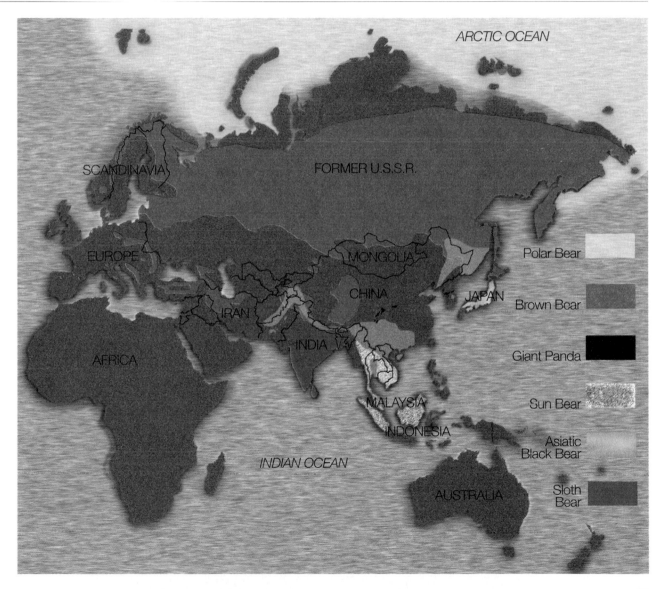

Further Reading

The Bamboo Bears by Clive Roots; Hyperion Press; Winnipeg; 1989.

Bear Attacks: Their Causes and Avoidance by Stephen Herrero; Nick Lyons Books; New York; 1985.

Bears: Majestic Creatures of the Wild, edited by Ian Stirling; Rodale Press, Emmaus; Pennsylvania; 1993.

Bears: Monarchs of the Northern Wilderness by Wayne Lynch; Grey-Stone Books, Douglas & McIntyre; Vancouver/Toronto; 1993.

Black Bear: Spirit of the Wilderness by Barbara Ford; Houghton Mifflin Company; Boston; 1981.

The Giant Pandas of Wolong by George Schaller, Hu Jinchu, Pan Wenshi and Zhu Jing; University of Chicago Press; Chicago; 1985.

Giving Voice to Bear: North American Indian Myths, Rituals, and Images of the Bear by David Rockwell; Roberts Rinehart Publishers; Niwot, Colorado; 1991.

The Great American Bear by Jeff Fair and Lynn Rogers; NorthWord Press; Minoqua, Wisconsin; 1990.

Great Bear Almanac by Gary Brown; Lyons and Burford Publishers; New York; 1993.

Polar Bears by Ian Stirling; University of Michigan Press; Ann Arbor; 1988.

Spirit Bear: Encounters With the White Bear of the Western Rainforest by Charles Russell; Key Porter Books; Toronto; 1994.

Index